The Science of Living Things

What is a Dinosaur?

Niki Walker & Bobbie Kalman

Crabtree Publishing Company
www.crabtreebooks.com

The Science of Living Things Series
A Bobbie Kalman Book

To Josh
with love and thanks for the Empire State Building

Editor-in-Chief
Bobbie Kalman

Writing team
Niki Walker
Bobbie Kalman

Managing editor
Lynda Hale

Researchers
Niki Walker
Allison Larin

Editing team
John Crossingham
Heather Levigne
Jane Lewis

Computer design
Niki Walker
Lynda Hale
Robert MacGregor (cover)

Production coordinator
Hannelore Sotzek

Consultant
Dr. Ronald Litwin is a professional geologist who has worked extensively on dinosaur-bearing rocks in North America.

Photographs and reproductions
Brian Franczak: pages 8, 9 (both), 15, 18-19, 21, 22, 25, 30 (top)
Mark Hallett Illustrations: front cover, pages 4, 14, 16, 17, 20, 23, 27
Douglas Henderson: page 26
Photo Researchers, Inc.: Francois Gohier: page 11 (bottom)
Photo Researchers, Inc./Science Photo Library:
    Victor Habbick Visions: page 29 (bottom); John Reader: page 11 (top); D. Van Ravenswaay: page 28
Digital Stock: title page

Illustrations
Trevor Morgan: pages 12-13 (hips)
Bonna Rouse: back cover (egg), pages 5, 6-7, 10, 12-13 (all except hips), 18, 24, 29 (top), 30 (bottom right)
Doug Swinamer: page 30 (bottom left)

Color separations and film
Dot 'n Line Image Inc.

Printer
Worzalla Publishing Company

Crabtree Publishing Company

PMB 16A	612 Welland Ave.,	73 Lime Walk
350 Fifth Ave.,	St. Catharines,	Headington
Suite 3308	Ontario, Canada	Oxford OX3 7AD
N.Y., N.Y. 10118	L2M 5V6	United Kingdom

Cataloging in Publication Data
Walker, Niki
    What is a dinosaur?

(The science of living things)
Includes index.

ISBN 0-86505-921-7 (library bound) ISBN 0-86505-949-7 (pbk.)
This book identifies what is and is not a dinosaur, discusses the physiology and behavior of various types, including stegosaurs, ankylosaurs, and ceratopsians, and introduces theories about their extinction.

1. Dinosaurs—Juvenile literature. [1. Dinosaurs.]
I. Kalman, Bobbie. II. Series: Kalman, Bobbie. Science of living things.

QE862.D5W22 1999   j567.9   LC 99-13157
                                                    CIP

Contents

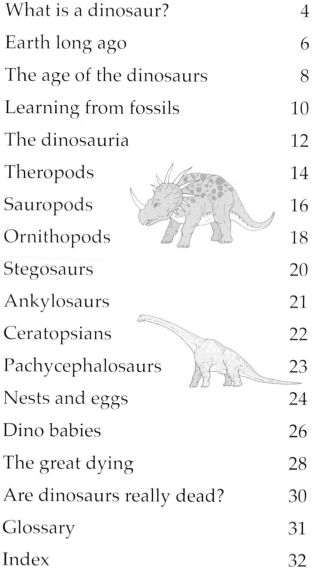
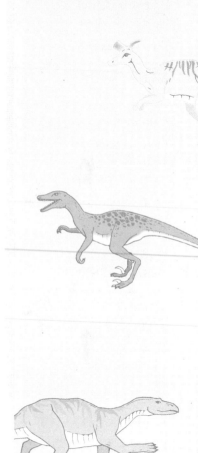

What is a dinosaur?

*Dinosaurs were either **bipedal** (two-legged), or **quadrupedal** (four-legged). Some were much bigger than an elephant, whereas others were as small as a chicken, even when fully grown!*

Dinosaurs were a group of ancient **reptiles** that lived on Earth for approximately 150 million years. The word dinosaur means "terrible lizard." Dinosaurs were named in 1842, before scientists discovered that they were not lizards.

There are both similarities and differences between dinosaurs and modern reptiles, such as crocodiles. Like other reptiles, dinosaurs had scaly skin, and they hatched from eggs. Scientists do not know if dinosaurs were **cold-blooded**, as today's reptiles are. A cold-blooded animal's body temperature changes with its surroundings. Some parts of dinosaur skeletons, such as their skull and legs, were different from those of other reptiles.

Dinosaurs, like birds, had ankle joints that forced their limbs to be vertical. Reptiles, such as the Komodo dragon above, have ankle joints that are more flexible. When they stand, their body is more horizontal.

pterosaurs

What isn't a dinosaur?

Dinosaurs were only one of many groups of prehistoric reptiles. Some of these reptiles, such as the pterosaurs, ichthyosaurs, and plesiosaurs, lived at the same time as dinosaurs, but they were not dinosaurs! Dinosaurs could not fly, as the pterosaurs did. No dinosaurs lived entirely in water, either, as the ichthyosaurs and plesiosaurs did.

ichthyosaurs

plesiosaurs

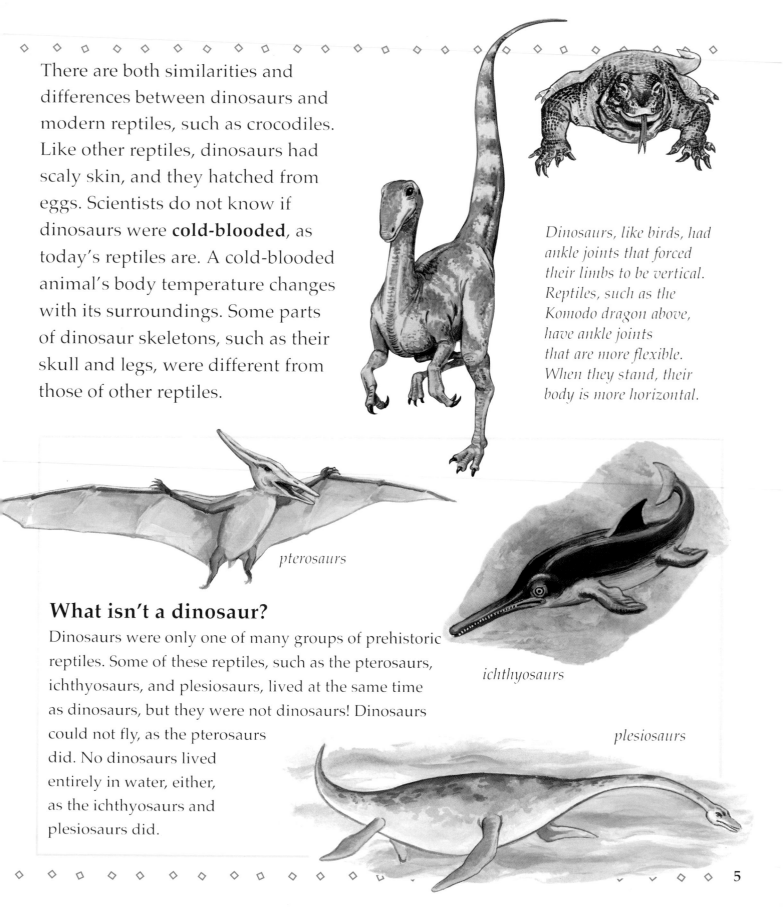

Earth long ago

Earth's history is divided into long blocks of time called **eras**. In each era, certain animals were most common. Dinosaurs lived during the Mesozoic era, also known as the Age of Reptiles and the Age of Dinosaurs.

Paleozoic era:

590-245 million years ago
The name Paleozoic means "ancient life." During this era, the most common animals were worms, fish, jellyfish, amphibians, and insects.

Triassic

Mesozoic era

245-65 million years ago
The name Mesozoic means "middle life." During this era, dinosaurs and other prehistoric reptiles were the most common animals. This era is subdivided into the **Triassic** period, the **Jurassic** period, and the **Cretaceous** period.

This diagram shows the creatures that were most common in the Paleozoic, Mesozoic, and Cenozoic eras of Earth's history. Most of Earth's history actually occurred before the Paleozoic era. Creatures that lived before the Paleozoic era had no shells for protection or body support and were therefore small in size.

Cenozoic era

65 million years ago to present
The name Cenozoic means "recent life." This era is also called the Age of Mammals because these animals became common at this time.

In the Triassic period, all land on Earth was part of a single continent called **Pangaea**. The first dinosaurs appeared in the late Triassic period.

Pangaea began to break apart during the Jurassic period, but the continents were connected by land bridges. Dinosaurs could still move over all the land.

By the Cretaceous period, Pangaea broke into the continents we know today. The dinosaur **species** on each continent were different from one another.

Triassic period: 245-205 million years ago

Jurassic period: 205-144 million years ago

Cretaceous period: 144-65 million years ago

Jurassic

Cretaceous

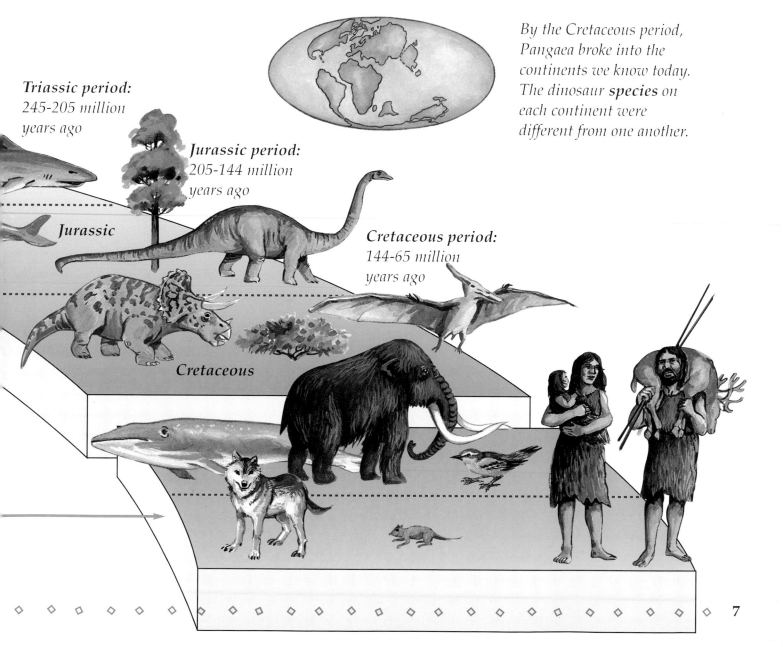

The age of the dinosaurs

Dinosaurs lived during the Mesozoic era. As Earth changed during this time (see globes on page 7), the dinosaurs **adapted**, or changed to suit their new environment. They **evolved**, which means their body and behavior changed so it would be easier for them to survive. Whereas some species of dinosaur died out quickly, others survived for two Mesozoic periods.

The Triassic period

The earliest dinosaurs discovered were small, bipedal **carnivores**, or meat eaters. *Coelophysis* (see page 15) is an example of these speedy hunters. The first known **herbivores**, or plant eaters, arrived soon after. They developed a larger body than the Triassic carnivores. All herbivores need a large stomach to help them digest the plants they eat. Their big size may also have given them protection from their small meat-eating enemies.

Many herbivores, such as these Plateosaurus, began walking on four legs because their long belly made it difficult for them to stand upright.

The Jurassic period

During the Jurassic period, Pangaea was breaking up. Shallow seas and new mountain ranges began to appear on the land. As the land changed, the weather changed as well. These changes caused plants and trees to grow and spread. Different species of dinosaurs evolved to live in these new forest and woodland habitats. Giant plant-eating dinosaurs appeared, and large meat-eating dinosaurs evolved to hunt them. Some plant eaters developed plates, spines, bony armor, and horns to protect themselves from carnivores.

Huge carnivores such as Ceratosaurus lived in the Jurassic period. Some of these dinosaurs were the largest meat eaters ever to live on land.

The Cretaceous period

By the Cretaceous period, the pieces of Pangaea had moved farther apart. Different dinosaurs evolved on each of the new continents. Flowering plants and small mammals also became more common. By the end of this period, however, all the dinosaurs disappeared. Scientists are not certain why. Turn to page 28 to read more about the end of the dinosaurs.

Triceratops were some of the last dinosaurs to walk the Earth 65 million years ago.

Learning from fossils

The information we have about dinosaurs comes from **fossils**. Fossils are the rocklike remains of animals that died and were quickly buried under layers of dirt and rock. Some of the best places to find dinosaur fossils are western North America, Argentina, China, Europe, Africa, and Mongolia.

Dinosaur fossils are divided into two groups. The first are **body fossils**, such as bones, skin, and eggs. The second type, called **trace fossils**, are the remains of an animal's activities or movements. They include nests and footprints. Even a dinosaur's dung can become a fossil, called a **coprolite**.

*A series of footprints called **trackways** can help show how a dinosaur moved.*

We will never really know how dinosaurs looked and lived. Fossils, such as this rare complete Iguanodon skeleton, are clues that help researchers guess what the dinosaurs were like. How do you think the dinosaurs lived?

Studying ancient life

The study of ancient plants and animals is called **paleontology**, and scientists who study ancient life are called **paleontologists**. Paleontologists have identified more than 800 species of dinosaurs from fossils. Some scientists believe that there are still many species to be discovered.

Piecing together the past

Paleontologists do not just identify dinosaurs—they study body and trace fossils to learn how the dinosaurs lived. They use information from modern animals to help them figure out how dinosaurs may have looked and lived. Paleontologists also need excellent science and math skills to **estimate**, or guess, a dinosaur's appearance, speed, or behavior.

*This group of paleontologists is carefully **excavating**, or digging out, fossils from rock.*

Lab workers use tiny drills, needles, and pins to clean fossils. Cleaning fossils can take years!

The dinosauria

All dinosaurs are placed into one group called the **dinosauria**. The dinosauria is divided into two smaller groups: the **saurischia** and the **ornithischia**.

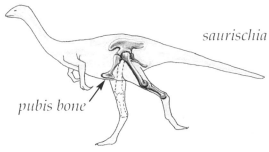

saurischia

pubis bone

Saurischians had a pubis hip bone that pointed downward and forward.

Saurischia

Saurischians are also known as lizard-hipped dinosaurs because their hip bones were arranged like those of a lizard. These hips may have been better suited to a heavier body weight.

The saurischia is made up of two smaller groups—the quick, fierce **theropods** and the giant **sauropods**. All carnivorous dinosaurs were theropods. The largest and heaviest dinosaurs to walk on Earth were sauropods.

Sauropods were quadrupedal plant eaters. They lived during the Jurassic and Cretaceous periods.

Brachiosaurus (sauropod)

Tyrannosaurus rex (theropod)

The first known dinosaurs were theropods. They lived throughout the Triassic, Jurassic, and Cretaceous periods.

Coelophysis (theropod)

Ornithischia

The **ornithischia**, or bird-hipped dinosaurs, had hip bones that were similar to those of modern birds. These herbivores had a longer stride than saurischian dinosaurs. Some were bipedal, and others were quadrupedal.

The ornithischia are divided into three smaller groups—the **ornithopods**, **thyreophorans**, and **marginocephalians**. Many ornithopods probably used their speed to escape predators. Thyreophorans and marginocephalians developed body armor to protect themselves.

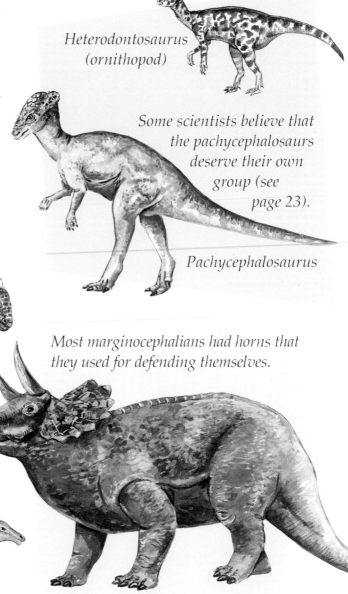

ornithischia

pubis bone

Ornithischia had a pubis that pointed downward and to the rear.

Heterodontosaurus (ornithopod)

Some scientists believe that the pachycephalosaurs deserve their own group (see page 23).

Pachycephalosaurus

Ankylosaurus (thyreophoran)

Thyreophorans had body armor to protect them from the teeth and claws of predators.

Most marginocephalians had horns that they used for defending themselves.

Stegosaurus (thyreophoran)

Triceratops (marginocephalian)

13

Theropods

There are more than 100 known types of theropods. Two groups within the theropods are the **carnosaurs** and **coelurosaurs**. Carnosaurs were large, heavy dinosaurs. Some carnosaurs were among the largest land carnivores ever! Coelurosaurs were small, light dinosaurs with hollow bones. Scientists believe that one group of coelurosaurs may be the ancestors of birds.

Carcharodontosaurus, a large carnosaur, defends its kill from a scavenger called Deltadromeus.

The theropod menu

Theropods were meat eaters. Carnosaurs fed mainly on other dinosaurs. Coelurosaurs probably ate lizards, mammals, insects, eggs, and baby dinosaurs. Scientists have found trackways suggesting that many theropods hunted in packs. Other theropods were **scavengers**. They did not kill their own food. Instead, they stole the prey of other animals or fed on dead animals that they found.

Made to hunt

Whether they were large or small, all theropods were built for hunting. They stood and walked on their hind legs, and they held their tail straight to help them balance. Theropods had two or three sharply clawed fingers on each hand. Almost all theropods had jaws filled with sharp, knifelike teeth.

(above) Small coelurosaurs such as Coelophysis probably lived and hunted in packs.

Sauropods

Sauropods were massive, long-bodied dinosaurs. Scientists believe that they traveled in large herds, grazing on plants. Fossils from about 60 types of sauropods have been found on every continent except Antarctica.

An ideal body

A sauropod's body may look clumsy to us, but it was well suited to its traveling, plant-eating lifestyle. Its thick legs easily supported the dinosaur's heavy body and were ideal for walking slowly over great distances. A sauropod's long neck and narrow head allowed it to reach the tops of trees and between branches. Most sauropods had poorly developed teeth and probably did not chew their food. Paleontologists believe that food was ground up by stones in the dinosaur's gut. The sauropod's long tail helped balance the rest of its body. Sauropods may have used their tail as a whip to defend themselves against predators. These giant dinosaurs also may have reared onto their hind legs and crushed their attacker with their forelegs.

Sauropods were the longest, tallest, and heaviest land animals that ever lived. Ultrasaurus stood 56 feet (17 m) tall. The giant Seismosaurus measured 130 feet (40 m) in length. It was the longest dinosaur known.

Ultrasaurus

Seismosaurus

Supersaurus

Diplodocus

Ornithopods

The name ornithopod means "bird feet." Small ornithopods (see page 13) probably ran quickly on two feet or all fours. Larger types, such as the hadrosaurs shown right, were probably quadrupedal. They moved more slowly.

Ornithopods were plant eaters that probably roamed in large herds. Since they had few defenses, living in herds made it easier for them to escape attackers.

(above) Some hadrosaurs had a hollow crest on top of their head. The crest may have helped hadrosaurs recognize other members of their herd, or they may have been used to make sounds.

Some hadrosaurs are also known as the duckbilled dinosaurs. Anototitian, shown here, had a wide, flat, toothless snout similar to that of a duck's bill.

Stegosaurs

The name stegosaur means "covered lizard." All stegosaurs belonged to the thyreophoran group. Bony plates or spines protected stegosaurs from enemies. When attacked, they may have swung their spiky tail like a club.

A stegosaur's plates also may have released extra body heat to help the dinosaur stay cool. These four-legged herbivores probably stood on their hind legs to reach taller plants. They used their small teeth to chew soft leaves.

There are over ten known kinds of stegosaurs. The best-known stegosaur is Stegosaurus. This dinosaur was the largest stegosaur and had the biggest plates.

Ankylosaurs

The name ankylosaur means "**fused lizard.**" Large plates of bone were fused, or joined, together over an ankylosaur's back and around its head. Imagine trying to bite through that! Some, such as the *Panoplosaurus* above, also had a large, bony club at the end of its tail. It may have used its club to swing at enemies. The ankylosaurs are a part of the thyreophoran group.

Ceratopsians

The name ceratopsian means "horned head." Many ceratopsians had sharp horns on their nose and above their eyes. All of them had a bony frill around the back of their head. The frill probably protected their neck and helped balance their long head. Ceratopsians were herbivores with a beaklike mouth. Their jaw opened and closed like the blades of scissors, slicing easily through leaves and other parts of plants.

Ceratopsians, including the Chasmosaurus shown left, were marginocephalians. There were over 20 types of ceratopsians.

Pachycephalosaurs

Pachycephalosaurs had a thick cap of bone at the top of their skull. This bony cap may have been used as a battering ram in contests to decide which pachycephalosaur was strongest. Some scientists believe pachycephalosaurs belong with the marginocephalians, whereas others think they were more closely related to the ornithopods. Other paleontologists argue that pachycephalosaurs do not belong to either group and should have their own group.

If pachycephalosaurs did head-butt, their thick skull shield could have helped protect their brain and spine from injury.

Nests and eggs

A male and female dinosaur mated in order to **reproduce**, or make babies. Paleontologists do not know much about how dinosaurs chose mates, but they do know that after mating, the female laid eggs just as reptiles and birds do today. People have found fossilized eggs from only a few types of dinosaurs.

Egg warmers

An egg must be kept warm for the baby inside to grow. Most dinosaurs built nests to help keep their eggs warm and safe. Nests were shallow holes scooped out of the ground and covered with plants. The plants rotted and gave off heat, keeping the eggs warm. Crocodiles today keep their eggs warm in the same way. Many dinosaurs were too heavy to **brood**, or sit on, their eggs to warm them as birds do.

Egg-ceptional eggs

Even though some dinosaurs were huge, their eggs were not. Dinosaur eggs ranged between one and twelve inches (2.5 and 30 cm) in length. The largest egg found so far belonged to a sauropod. It was one foot (30 cm) long and ten inches (25 cm) across.

Baby dinosaurs had to grow a lot before they reached the size of their parents! This sauropod was about 15 inches (37.5 cm) long when it hatched. By the time is was an adult, it was almost 45 feet (13.7 m) long.

The dinosaurs shown here are called Maiasaura, meaning "mother lizard." They were the first known examples of dinosaurs that nurtured their young.

Dino Babies

Newly hatched dinosaurs were called **hatchlings**. Some dinosaurs hatched with well-developed legs and left the nest almost immediately to find food. Many hatchlings, however, were too weak to leave their nest. Scientists believe that the parents cared for these helpless dinosaur babies.

Paleontologists have found large groups of dinosaur nests. It is likely that a group of dinosaurs could care for their hatchlings better than a lone pair of parents. While some parents searched for food, others guarded the nest site.

Get in the ring!

Paleontologists believe that ceratopsians may have defended their hatchlings by forming a large circle around them. With each dinosaur facing outward, a predator met with sharp horns from any direction it attacked. Scientists have also found trace fossils suggesting that adult sauropods surrounded the young members of their herd as they traveled. In the center of the herd, young sauropods were safer from predators.

The great dying

Dinosaurs lived on Earth for over 150 million years—longer than any other group of animals has lived on the planet. About 65 million years ago, however, something happened that caused the dinosaurs to become **extinct**, or to die out.

Not just the dinosaurs died. More than half of all animal species on Earth at that time died out! Scientists have called this occurrence "the Cretaceous extinction event." There are many different **theories**, or ideas, about what caused this great extinction.

Killer crash

A recent theory is that a huge **asteroid**, or space rock, hit Earth. Scientists have found some evidence that the crash happened near the end of the Cretaceous period. The asteroid exploded when it hit Earth, sending a large cloud of dust and rocks into the air. The cloud was so thick that it blocked out most of the sun. The crash also caused fires, storms, and volcanic eruptions. Plants died, and the plant eaters starved to death. Carnivores that fed on the herbivores died from starvation as well. Many questions still remain about this theory.

People once thought that mammals that fed on dinosaur eggs ate so many that the dinosaurs died out. Few people now accept this theory.

Death by weather

Some scientists believe that the dinosaurs were not killed by the asteroid and that most were gone before the crash. They argue that the dinosaurs slowly died out because **climates** became cooler toward the end of the Cretaceous period. Which theory do you think best explains the Cretaceous extinction event? Do you have your own theory?

Are dinosaurs really dead?

Many paleontologists argue that dinosaurs never really died out, but evolved as birds. These scientists believe that birds are the descendants of a group of coelurosaurs. The bodies of birds and coelurosaurs are alike in many ways. For example, they have hollow bones and similar skulls, legs, and feet. The ancestors of birds were covered in scales, just as coelurosaurs were. Aside from the scales on their legs and feet, however, birds' scales have evolved into feathers.

Scientists have found fossils of several dinosaurs that were covered with small, primitive feathers.

Ancient wings

The fossil of a creature known as *Archaeopteryx* is an important link between dinosaurs and birds.

Scientists believe it may be the earliest known bird. *Archaeopteryx* had a skeleton much like that of a coelurosaur, but its body was covered with feathers. Its name means "ancient wing."

Glossary

ancestor An animal from which similar animals have descended

ankylosaur A dinosaur with protective bone plates covering the body and head

bipedal An animal that walks on two legs

carnivore An animal that eats mainly meat

carnosaur A large meat-eating, bipedal dinosaur

ceratopsian A dinosaur with a protective bony frill; most have horns

coelurosaur A small meat-eating, bipedal dinosaur

cold-blooded Describing an animal whose body temperature changes with the temperature of its surroundings

coprolite Animal waste that has turned into a fossil

Cretaceous The third Mesozoic period

evolve To change over a long period of time

excavate To dig something out of the ground

extinct Describing a species of animal or plant that is no longer living

fossil A living thing, or mark made by a living thing, that has hardened into rock over time

hadrosaur A large bird-hipped dinosaur that walked on two or four legs

ichthyosaur A early marine reptile whose name means "fish lizard"

Jurassic The second Mesozoic period

marginocephalian A bird-hipped dinosaur with head armor, such as horns or a bony frill

mate A partner an animal needs to help make babies

Mesozoic The era of time on Earth in which dinosaurs existed and became extinct

ornithischia A group of dinosaurs that had hip bones similar to those of modern birds

ornithopod A type of bird-hipped dinosaur

pachycephalosaur A bird-hipped dinosaur with a thick, bony skull cap

paleontology The study of prehistoric life

plesiosaur A marine reptile with a long neck, small head, and four flippers

prehistoric The time in Earth's history before humans existed

pterosaur A flying reptile with large wings made of membrane, or skin

quadrupedal An animal that walks on four legs

saurischia A group of dinosaurs that had hip bones similar to those of modern reptiles

sauropod A giant reptile-hipped dinosaur with a long neck and tail

species A group of similar animals whose offspring are able to make babies

stegosaur A dinosaur with large protective spines or plates on its back

theory An idea used to explain why or how something happened

theropod A meat-eating, bipedal dinosaur

thyreophoran A bird-hipped dinosaur with body armor, plates or spines

Triassic The first Mesozoic period

Index

amphibians 6
ankylosaurs 21
Archaeopteryx 30
armor 13
babies 15, 24, 26-27
birds 5, 13, 14, 18, 24, 30
bones 10, 13, 14, 20, 21, 22, 23, 30
Brachiosaurus 12
carnivores 8, 9, 12, 14, 15, 29
carnosaurs 14, 15
Cenozoic 6
ceratopsians 22, 27
Ceratosaurus 9, 20
Chasmosaurus 22
Coelophysis 12, 15
coelurosaurs 14, 15, 30
continents 7, 9, 16
Cretaceous 6, 7, 9, 12, 28, 29
crocodiles 5, 24
defenses *see* protection
Earth 4, 6-7, 8, 9, 17, 28, 29
eggs 5, 10, 15, 24-25, 29
enemies *see* predators
eras 6, 8
extinction 28-29
feet 18, 30
fish 6
food 15, 17, 26
footprints *see* trackways
fossils 10-11, 16, 24, 25, 27
hadrosaurs 18, 19

hatchlings *see* babies
head 17, 18, 21, 22, 23
herbivores 8, 9, 12, 13, 17, 18, 20, 22, 29
herds 18, 27
hips 12, 13
horns 13, 22, 27
ichthyosaurs 5
Iguanodon 10
insects 6, 15
Jurassic 6, 7, 9, 12
legs 4, 5, 8, 13, 15, 17, 18, 20, 26, 30
lizards 4, 12, 15, 20, 21, 25
Maiasaura 25, 26
mammals 6, 9, 13, 15, 29
marginocephalians 13, 22, 23
Mesozoic 6, 8-9
neck 17, 20, 22
nests 10, 24-25, 26
ornithischia 12, 13
ornithopods 13, 18-19, 23
pachycephalosaurs 13, 23
packs 15
paleontologists 11, 17, 21, 23, 24, 26, 27, 30
Paleozoic 6
Pangaea 7, 9
parents 24, 25, 26
plants 8, 9, 11, 12, 16, 17, 18, 20, 22, 24, 29
Plateosaurus 8

plates 20, 21
plesiosaurs 5
predators 13, 17, 18, 20, 21, 27
protection 8, 9, 13, 17, 18, 20, 23
pterosaurs 5
reptiles 4, 5, 6, 12, 24
saurischia 12
sauropods 9, 12, 16-17, 24, 27
scales 5, 30
scavengers 14, 15
scientists 4, 5, 6, 9, 11, 13, 14, 15, 16, 23, 26, 27, 28, 29, 30
Seismosaurus 16, 17
skeletons 5, 10, 30
skin 10
skulls 23, 30
species 7, 11, 19
spines 20
stegosaurs 20
Stegosaurus 13, 20
stomach 8
tails 15, 17, 20, 21
teeth 13, 15, 17, 19, 20
theory 28, 29
theropods 12, 14-15
thyreophorans 13, 20, 21
trackways 10, 15
Triassic 6, 7, 8, 12
Triceratops 9, 13, 27
Tyrannosaurus rex 12, 27

3 4 5 6 7 8 9 0 Printed in the U.S.A. 8 7 6 5 4 3 2 1